Word Family Stories

★ **31** Delightful Mini-Books with Humorous, Decodable Story Texts

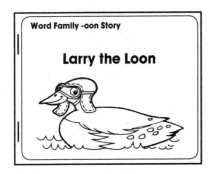

Word Family -oon Story

Larry the Loon

by
Kathryn Wheeler

Word Family -op Story

The New Shop

illustrated by
Vanessa Countryman

Word Family -ig Story

Big Pig

Word Family -amp Story

Save Me from Camp!

Word Family -ee Story

Lee the Bee

Publisher
Key Education Publishing Company, LLC
Minneapolis, Minnesota

CONGRATULATIONS ON YOUR PURCHASE OF A KEY EDUCATION PRODUCT!

The editors at Key Education are former teachers who bring experience, enthusiasm, and quality to each and every product. Thousands of teachers have looked to the staff at Key Education for new and innovative resources to make their work more enjoyable and rewarding. We are committed to developing educational materials that will assist teachers in building a strong and developmentally appropriate curriculum for young children.

PLAN FOR GREAT TEACHING EXPERIENCES WHEN YOU USE EDUCATIONAL MATERIALS FROM KEY EDUCATION PUBLISHING COMPANY, LLC!

CONTENTS

HOW TO USE THIS BOOK

Word Family Stories contains 31 delightful reproducible mini-books with humorous, decodable story texts. These stories will introduce children to 31 word families, unlocking the key to dozens of words that will become instantly recognizable.

Why are word families important? Word families, or phonograms, are the building blocks of words. Each phonogram is the remainder of the word left when the opening sound is taken away. By practicing reading within a word family, students can boost their word power and can decode words readily. As children learn that words contain chunks of letters that create recognizable sounds, their reading confidence grows.

Directions: Reproduce a storybook for each child. Cut out the pages along the dashed lines and then collate and staple them together in numerical order.

For specific reading suggestions and activities, turn to the last page of each mini-book for additional ideas and the word family list.

CREDITS

Author: Kathryn Wheeler
Publisher: Sherrill B. Flora
Inside Illustrations: Vanessa Countryman
Creative Director: Annette Hollister-Papp
Cover Design: Mary Eden
Project Director: Debra Pressnall

Key Education welcomes manuscripts and product ideas from teachers. For a copy of our submission guidelines, please send a self-addressed, stamped envelope to:
Key Education Publishing Company, LLC
Acquisitions Department
9601 Newton Avenue South
Minneapolis, Minnesota 55431

ISBN: 978-1-933052-33-5
Word Family Stories
Copyright © 2007 Key Education Publishing Company, LLC
Minneapolis, Minnesota 55431

Word Family -ag Story

Helping Aunt Ag

Mom sent us to help Aunt Ag.
But Aunt Ag likes to nag.

2

"Pick up that rag!" said Aunt Ag.
"Time for work!"

3

"Drag that bag with the tag out,"
said Aunt Ag. "Hurry!"

4

6

"Now climb the crag. Put up the flag," Aunt Ag said.

8

NOTES TO TEACHERS AND PARENTS

DIRECTIONS TO MAKE THE BOOK: Copy the storybook for each student. Color and cut out the pages along the dashed lines. Staple them together in numerical order.

BEFORE READING

1. Read the following words from the word family -*ag* that appear in the story: *Ag, nag, rag, bag, tag, lag, gag(s), brag, crag, flag, sag.*

2. Review any unfamiliar words in the story.

AFTER READING

1. Discuss the story. What -*ag* words do the students remember?
2. Look through the story. Find and circle each -*ag* word.

MORE ACTIVITIES

1. What works better than being a nag? Talk about it.
2. Read a tall tale. Does the character brag? Make up something to brag about, as if you were in a tall tale.

5

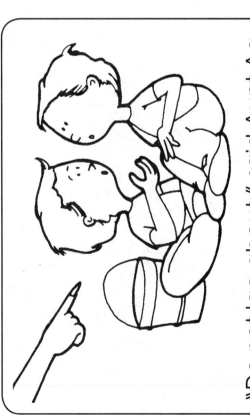

"Do not lag about," said Aunt Ag. "No gags! Do not brag!"

7

"Don't sag when you stand," said Aunt Ag. But we are tired. It is hard work helping Aunt Ag!

Dan Buys Bran

Dan got a bag of bran.

He put the bran into his van.

Dan's plan was to bake muffins with the bran.

6

"Now I need a fan!" said Dan, "I can hardly carry this bran!"

8

NOTES TO TEACHERS AND PARENTS

DIRECTIONS TO MAKE THE BOOK: Copy the storybook for each student. Color and cut out the pages along the dashed lines. Staple them together in numerical order.

BEFORE READING
1. Read the following words from the word family –an that appear in the story: *Dan, bran, plan, ran, fan, can, clan, pan.*
2. Review any unfamiliar words in the story.

AFTER READING
1. Discuss the story. What –an words do the students remember?
2. Look through the story. Find and circle each –an word.

MORE ACTIVITIES
1. Brainstorm a list of other words that belong to the –an family (*man, tan, scan, span*, etc.). See if the students can help you make up another story about Dan using the new words.
2. As a class, make bran muffins if you have kitchen facilities. (Check for food allergies first!) Enjoy the muffins during snack time.

5

Oh, no! The bran fell out of the van. Dan ran.

7

Dan got back his bran. Dan's whole clan came for a big pan of bran muffins.

The bat took my hat.
Did you see that?

Now my hat and the bat are
inside Nat the Cat!

Word Family -at Story

The Bat,
the Cat,
and
My Hat

Nat the Cat ate the bat.
Nat is getting fat.

6

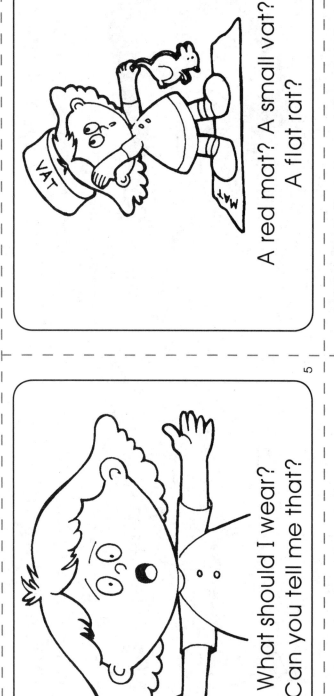

A red mat? A small vat?
A flat rat?

5

What should I wear?
Can you tell me that?

8

NOTES TO TEACHERS AND PARENTS

DIRECTIONS TO MAKE THE BOOK: Copy the storybook for each student. Color and cut out the pages along the dashed lines. Staple them together in numerical order.

BEFORE READING

1. Read the following words from the word family *-at* that appear in the story: *that, bat, hat, Nat, cat, fat, mat, vat, rat.*

2. Review any unfamiliar words in the story.

AFTER READING

1. Discuss the story. What *-at* words do the students remember?

2. Look through the story. Find and circle each *-at* word.

MORE ACTIVITIES

1. Design hats! Use paper plates as a base—glue or staple on cutout paper flowers. Use markers or crayons to color.

2. Have the students draw pictures of *-at* words on index cards. Make flash cards.

7

Maybe, I should wear Nat the
Cat as my new hat!

I can't stand camp.

Our lamp will not light.
It is too damp.

Word Family -amp Story

Save
Me from
Camp!

My group is called "The
Champs." The tent is damp.

Ow! Now my leg has a cramp!

6

NOTES TO TEACHERS AND PARENTS

DIRECTIONS TO MAKE THE BOOK: Copy the storybook for each student. Color and cut out the pages along the dashed lines. Staple them together in numerical order.

BEFORE READING
1. Read the following words from the word family -amp that appear in the story: camp, damp, champ(s), lamp, tramp, cramp, stamp.
2. Review any unfamiliar words in the story.

AFTER READING
1. Discuss the story. What -amp words do the students remember?
2. Look through the story. Find and circle each -amp word.

MORE ACTIVITIES
1. Write a story about a person who likes camp. Try to include as many -amp words as possible.
2. Draw stamps for a camp. Decorate them with tents, pine trees, canoes, and so on.

8

We tramp and tramp in the woods. Why?

5

Please give me a stamp. I will write to my mom. I will say, "Save me from this camp!"

CHAMPS

7

Someone knocked on the door.
"Bang, bang, bang!"

It was the whole gang. They
wanted to hang out.

Word Family -ang Story

The Whole Gang

Fang, our dog, sprang up.
He barked.

6

We sang songs. The whole gang sang. We were loud!

8

NOTES TO TEACHERS AND PARENTS

DIRECTIONS TO MAKE THE BOOK: Copy the storybook for each student. Color and cut out the pages along the dashed lines. Staple them together in numerical order.

BEFORE READING ——————————————
1. Read the following words from the word family *-ang* that appear in the story: *bang, Fang, sprang, gang, hang, Chang, sang, rang, clang.*
2. Review any unfamiliar words in the story.

AFTER READING ——————————————
1. Discuss the story. What *-ang* words do the students remember?
2. Look through the story. Find and circle each *-ang* word.

MORE ACTIVITIES
1. Lots of *-ang* words are for noises: *bang, clang, rang, sang, twang.* Have students make each of these noises. How are the noises the same? How are they different?
2. What are the names of students' pets? Make a list. Do any of the names belong in the *-ang* word family?

5

"What should we do?" asked Chang.

7

Chang rang a bell. "Clang, clang, clang!" Fang barked. The whole gang had a great time.

2

Frank and Hank had to go
to the bank.

4

A firefighter saved them
with a plank.

Word Family -ank Story

A Trip to the Bank

1

3

They set out in a boat.
But then it sank.

6

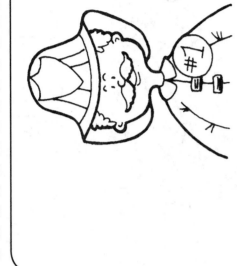

"You were brave to yank us out with that plank."

5

"Thank you! Thank you!" said Hank and Frank.

7

The firefighter drove Hank and Frank to the bank. The fire truck bell went "CLANK, CLANK, CLANK."

8

NOTES TO TEACHERS AND PARENTS

DIRECTIONS TO MAKE THE BOOK: Copy the storybook for each student. Color and cut out the pages along the dashed lines. Staple them together in numerical order.

BEFORE READING
1. Read the following words from the word family -ank that appear in the story: Frank, Hank, bank, sank, plank, thank, yank, clank.
2. Review any unfamiliar words in the story.

AFTER READING
1. Discuss the story. What -ank words do the students remember?
2. Look through the story. Find and circle each -ank word.

MORE ACTIVITIES
1. Set up a bank with play money. Have the students take turns going to the bank and being the bank clerk.
2. Play charades with -ank words and see if students can guess them. Act out "drank," "crank," "yank," "blank," and so on.

2

I am going to make a cake for Jake.

4

I take a table down to the lake.

1

Jake's Cake

3

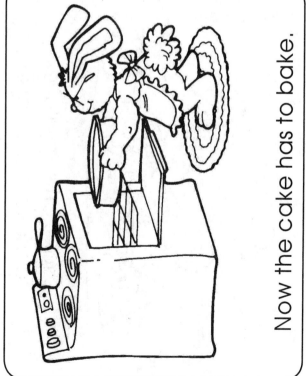

Now the cake has to bake.

6

Jake the Snake is the first to get to the lake.

8

NOTES TO TEACHERS AND PARENTS

DIRECTIONS TO MAKE THE BOOK: Copy the storybook for each student. Color and cut out the pages along the dashed lines. Staple them together in numerical order.

BEFORE READING

1. Read the following words from the word family -*ake* that appear in the story: *make, cake, bake, lake, shake, flake(s), Jake, snake.*
2. Review any unfamiliar words in the story.

AFTER READING

1. Discuss the story. What -*ake* words do the students remember?
2. Look through the story. Find and circle each -*ake* word.

MORE ACTIVITIES

1. What presents could you bring for Jake the Snake? Draw a picture of your present.
2. Vote for students' favorite cakes. Make a chart or graph to show how everyone voted.

5

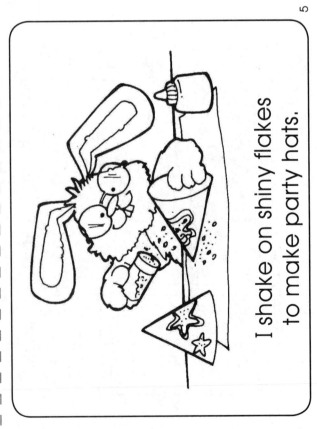

I shake on shiny flakes to make party hats.

7

I take the cake down to the lake. Party time!

Jill made a cape out of lots and lots of tape.

Jill's cape makes her look like a grape!

Word Family -ape Story

Jill's Cape

She worked hard to get the cape to drape.

6

When Jill walks, the cape sticks and scrapes.

8

NOTES TO TEACHERS AND PARENTS

DIRECTIONS TO MAKE THE BOOK: Copy the storybook for each student. Color and cut out the pages along the dashed lines. Staple them together in numerical order.

BEFORE READING
1. Read the following words from the word family *-ape* that appear in the story: *cape, tape, drape, grape, gape, scrape(s), shape.*
2. Review any unfamiliar words in the story.

AFTER READING
1. Discuss the story. What *-ape* words do the students remember?
2. Look through the story. Find and circle each *-ape* word.

MORE ACTIVITIES
1. Make a cape in class out of crepe paper streamers attached to a construction paper "collar." Have the students take turns wearing the cape and pretending to be Jill.
2. Look at different kinds of tape: Scotch, masking, duct, etc. Which one is the stickiest? Which one is the strongest?

5

I think people will gape at Jill's sticky cape.

7

When the wind blows, her cape changes shape! HELP!

Let's make a date to see
the state of the attic.

What's inside the crate?
I hate to guess!

Word Family -ate Story

Attic Date

What was the fate of the
old bear on this crate?

6

Look at that old plate by the grate. And here's a skate!

8

NOTES TO TEACHERS AND PARENTS

DIRECTIONS TO MAKE THE BOOK: Copy the storybook for each student. Color and cut out the pages along the dashed lines. Staple them together in numerical order.

BEFORE READING --------
1. Read the following words from the word family *-ate* that appear in the story: *date, state, crate, fate, hate, Kate, plate, grate, skate, late.*
2. Review any unfamiliar words in the story.

AFTER READING --------
1. Discuss the story. What *-ate* words do the students remember?
2. Look through the story. Find and circle each *-ate* word.

MORE ACTIVITIES --------
1. Draw a picture of another *-ate* treasure that the kids could find in the attic.
2. Make memory crates out of shoeboxes. Have the students put in things that tell something about themselves—the kind of crate that might someday be in an attic.

5

Look! It's Aunt Kate!

7

We're late! Let's take Aunt Kate, the plate, and the skate with us.

2

My sister Rain is a pain!

4

Sometimes, I wish Rain was a sack of grain.

Word Family -ain Story

Rain the Pain

1

3

Rain is the main reason that I want to move to Spain.

6

"I can't stand the strain of Rain," I told my mother. "She broke my favorite chain!"

5

I would load her on a train. "Good-bye, Rain!"

8

NOTES TO TEACHERS AND PARENTS

DIRECTIONS TO MAKE THE BOOK: Copy the storybook for each student. Color and cut out the pages along the dashed lines. Staple them together in numerical order.

BEFORE READING
1. Read the following words from the word family *-ain* that appear in the story: *Rain, pain, main, Spain, grain, train, strain, chain, plain.*
2. Review any unfamiliar words in the story.

AFTER READING
1. Discuss the story. What *-ain* words do the students remember?
2. Look through the story. Find and circle each *-ain* word.

MORE ACTIVITIES
1. What *-ain* words could describe people? As a class, brainstorm a list. (Possible answers include *pain, vain, brain, plain,* etc.)
2. Write another story about Rain and her sister.

7

It's plain that Rain is going to stay. She will stay a pain, too!

One day, a silly blue jay wanted to play.

But a truck took all the hay away!

Word Family -ay Story

A Silly Blue Jay

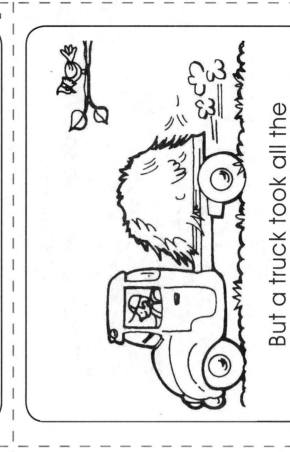

First, he went to play in some hay.

6

"I may play in the spray,"
said the jay.

5

Next, that jay found the way
to the bay.

NOTES TO TEACHERS AND PARENTS

DIRECTIONS TO MAKE THE BOOK: Copy the storybook for each student. Color and cut out the pages along the dashed lines. Staple them together in numerical order.

BEFORE READING
1. Read the following words from the word family -ay that appear in the story: *jay, day, play, hay, away, way, bay, spray, day.*
2. Review any unfamiliar words in the story.

AFTER READING
1. Discuss the story. What -ay words do the students remember?
2. Look through the story. Find and circle each -ay word.

MORE ACTIVITIES
1. Brainstorm other ways that the blue jay could play. Use other -ay words. Examples: He could play with clay. He could pay to go to a movie. He could make a tray of cookies.
2. Talk about the students' favorite ways to play.

8

7

Look out, blue jay!
Oh, what a day!

I took my pet Chet to the vet on my jet.

Chet needed a treat after he met with the vet.

Word Family -et Story

Chet Visits the Vet

I am willing to bet that no other pet yet gets to jet to the vet!

6

Chet got wet after I set him on the sand.

8

NOTES TO TEACHERS AND PARENTS

DIRECTIONS TO MAKE THE BOOK: Copy the storybook for each student. Color and cut out the pages along the dashed lines. Staple them together in numerical order.

BEFORE READING

1. Read the following words from the word family -*et* that appear in the story: *Chet, pet, vet, jet, bet, yet, get[s], met, wet, set, fret.*
2. Review any unfamiliar words in the story.

AFTER READING

1. Discuss the story. What -*et* words do the students remember?
2. Look through the story. Find and circle each -*et* word.

MORE ACTIVITIES

1. Talk about vets. Why are there special doctors for animals?
2. Make paper "jet" planes and have a flying contest.

5

So I took Chet in the jet to the beach.

7

Don't fret, Chet! I bet you will be dry soon!

2

"Nell, we must sell our magic shell," said Mama.

4

Nell reached the dell. She smiled and yelled, "This is swell!"

1

Word Family -ell Story

Nell Sells the Shell

3

"Ride the cow with the bell to the town in the dell. Sell this shell well," she told Nell.

6

"I will sell the shell and the cow with the bell. Then I will tell Mama," Nell said.

8

NOTES TO TEACHERS AND PARENTS

DIRECTIONS TO MAKE THE BOOK: Copy the storybook for each student. Color and cut out the pages along the dashed lines. Staple them together in numerical order.

BEFORE READING
1. Read the following words from the word family -ell that appear in the story: Nell, sell, shell, bell, dell, well, dwell, swell, tell, yell[ed].
2. Review any unfamiliar words in the story.

AFTER READING
1. Discuss the story. What -ell words do the students remember?
2. Look through the story. Find and circle each -ell word.

MORE ACTIVITIES
1. Make up a story about Nell and the magic well. What does the water do? Use other -ell words to tell the story.
2. Make a list of simple geographic terms, such as dell, lake, hill, sea, etc. Identify the word family for each term.

5

"I want to dwell in this pretty dell for the rest of my life," said Nell.

7

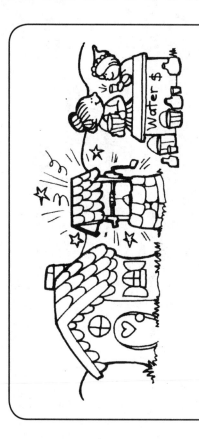

Nell bought a house with a magic well. She and Mama sold water in the dell!

"I have the best nest in the West," bragged the blue jay.

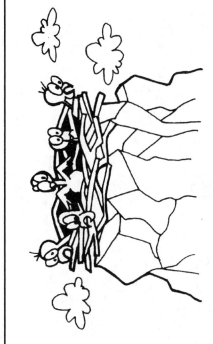

"Your nest is on the crest of that hill," said the blue jay. "A big wind could put your nest to the test."

Word Family -est Story

The Best Nest

"Ha!" said the eagle. "You jest! My nest is the best!"

6

"Don't be a pest!" snapped
the jay with zest.

8

5

"Well, your nest is so small it
would fit in my vest!" said the
eagle. "It would never pass
a test for the best."

7

Each bird was sure that her nest
was the best.

A little mouse named Squeak wanted to sneak outside.

Oh, no! An owl heard Squeak. He has Squeak in his beak!

Word Family -eak Story

Squeak and the Owl

"Squeak, squeak!" he bragged. "I will streak across the field!"

6

Things look bleak for Squeak.
Squeak starts to speak.

8

NOTES TO TEACHERS AND PARENTS

DIRECTIONS TO MAKE THE BOOK: Copy the storybook for each student. Color and cut out the pages along the dashed lines. Staple them together in numerical order.

BEFORE READING ————————————
1. Read the following words from the word family -eak that appear in the story: *Squeak, sneak, streak, beak, peak, bleak, speak, weak.*
2. Review any unfamiliar words in the story.

AFTER READING ————————————
1. Discuss the story. What -eak words do the students remember?
2. Look through the story. Find and circle each -eak word.

MORE ACTIVITIES
1. Make up a story using -eak action words (verbs): *leak, creak, sneak, speak, squeak, streak, tweak,* etc.
2. Learn more about owls. Find out how they use their beaks, eyes, and feet to catch food.

5

The owl flies away
to a high peak.

7

"I am small and weak. I am not good to eat. Let me go!"
The owl drops Squeak on the top of the peak. He is safe!

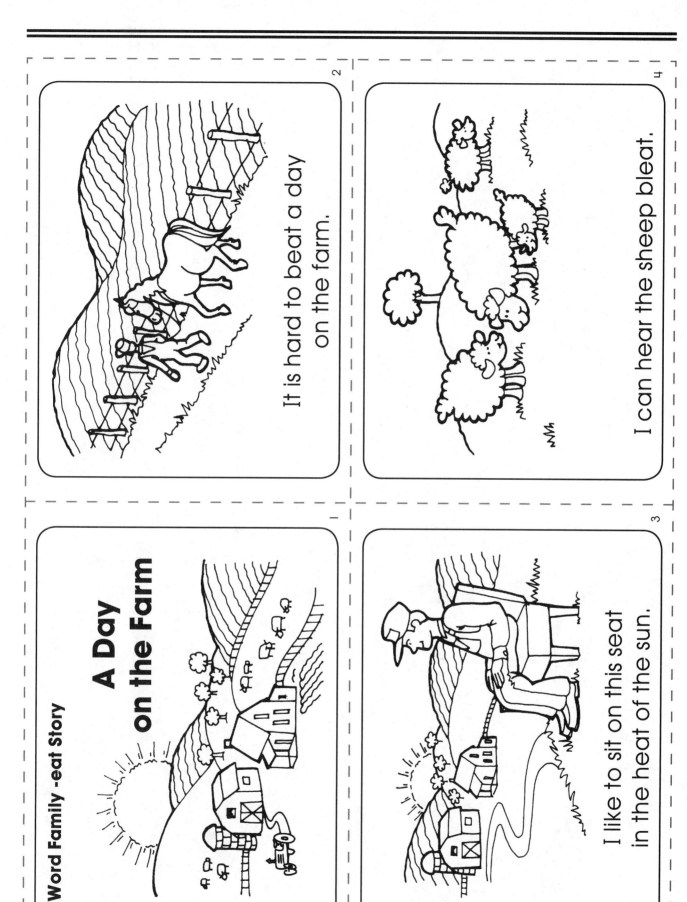

2

It is hard to beat a day
on the farm.

4

I can hear the sheep bleat.

Word Family -eat Story

A Day
on the Farm

1

3

I like to sit on this seat
in the heat of the sun.

6

My wife is cooking meat over the fire. We will eat it later.

NOTES TO TEACHERS AND PARENTS

DIRECTIONS TO MAKE THE BOOK: Copy the storybook for each student. Color and cut out the pages along the dashed lines. Staple them together in numerical order.

BEFORE READING

1. Read the following words from the word family *-eat* that appear in the story: *beat, seat, heat, bleat, wheat, meat, eat, treat, neat.*
2. Review any unfamiliar words in the story.

AFTER READING

1. Discuss the story. What *-eat* words do the students remember?
2. Look through the story. Find and circle each *-eat* word.

MORE ACTIVITIES

1. What are the students' favorite things to eat? Make a chart of their favorites.
2. Sheep bleat. What are the sounds that other farm animals make?

8

5

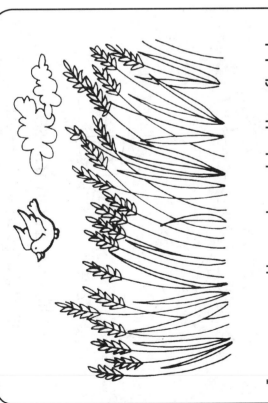

I can see the wheat in the fields.

7

What a treat to watch my neat, quiet farm!

Word Family -ee Story

Lee the Bee

Lee the Bee wanted to flee the hive.

"I am free!" cried Lee with glee.

"I can see the world. I can sleep in a tree!"

6

First, Lee went on
a shopping spree.

8

NOTES TO TEACHERS AND PARENTS

DIRECTIONS TO MAKE THE BOOK: Copy the storybook for each student. Color and cut out the pages along the dashed lines. Staple them together in numerical order.

BEFORE READING
1. Read the following words from the word family -ee that appear in the story: *Lee, bee, flee, free, glee, see, tree, wee, spree, tee, knee.*
2. Review any unfamiliar words in the story.

AFTER READING
1. Discuss the story. What -ee words do the students remember?
2. Look through the story. Find and circle each -ee word.

MORE ACTIVITIES
1. Learn the Mother Goose rhyme "The Fly Has Married the Bumblebee."
2. Bring in a jar of honey for the students to taste. (Check for food allergies first!) Talk about how bees make honey.

5

"I am free to build
my own, wee home."

7

She bought honey, three tee
shirts, and bee's knee socks!

Word Family -eed Story

Mystery Seed

I planted a seed.

Will my seed grow into a flower?
Will it be a reed?

What does it need?
It needs sun and water.

6

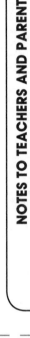

Oh, no! It is a weed!
We do not need weeds.

8

NOTES TO TEACHERS AND PARENT

DIRECTIONS TO MAKE THE BOOK: Copy the storybook for each student. Color and cut out the pages along the dashed lines. Staple them together in numerical order.

BEFORE READING
1. Read the following words from the word family *-eed* that appear in the story: *seed, need, reed, speed, weed, deed, feed.*
2. Review any unfamiliar words in the story.

AFTER READING
1. Discuss the story. What *-eed* words do the students remember?
2. Look through the story. Find and circle each *-eed* word.

MORE ACTIVITIES
1. Plant "mystery" seeds. Give them sunshine and water. What kind of plants will grow?
2. Read a children's gardening book. Why is it important to pull up weeds?

5

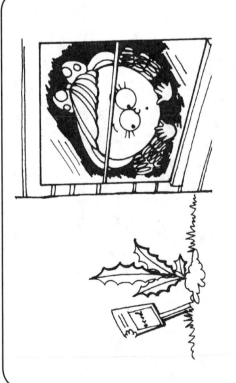

Look! My seed has grown
with speed.

7

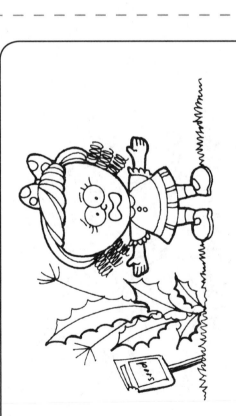

What a sad deed to feed the
seed of a weed!

2

Five sheep rode down the road in a jeep.

4

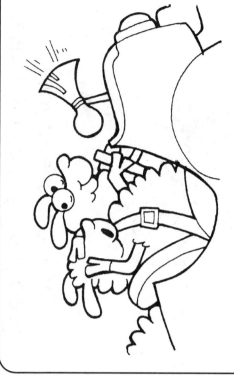

The second sheep cried, "This hill is too steep!"

Sheep Road Trip

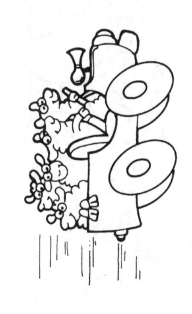

1

3

One sheep honked the horn. "Beep, beep!"

39

Word Family Stories

6

The fourth sheep yelled, "Keep your hoof on the brake!"

8

NOTES TO TEACHERS and PARENTS

DIRECTIONS TO MAKE THE BOOK: Copy the storybook for each student. Color and cut out the pages along the dashed lines. Staple them together in numerical order.

BEFORE READING
1. Read the following words from the word family -*eep* that appear in the story: *sheep, jeep*, beep, steep, creep, keep, weep, sleep.*

   (*Jeep is a registered trademark of DaimlerChrysler Corporation.)
2. Review any unfamiliar words in the story.

AFTER READING
1. Discuss the story. What -*eep* words do the students remember?
2. Look through the story. Find and circle each -*eep* word.

MORE ACTIVITIES
1. Make Sheep Road Trip pictures. Draw the jeep and glue on cotton balls to add the sheep.
2. Ask the students to tell about road trips they have taken with their families. Did they go down steep hills? Did they see sheep in the fields? Did they beep the horn?

5

The third sheep said, "Creep down this steep hill."

7

The fifth sheep sobbed, "I will weep if we cannot sleep soon!"

2

Big Pig drove to town in his bright red rig.

4

Then he danced a jig!
Well done, Big Pig!

Word Family -ig Story

Big Pig

1

3

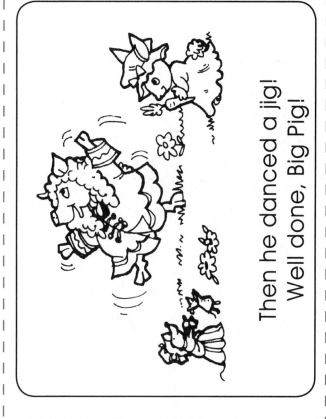

He went out to dine.
He ate a fig off a twig.

6

He went out to buy a new wig.

5

Big Pig put on a sprig of holly.

8

NOTES TO TEACHERS AND PARENTS

DIRECTIONS TO MAKE THE BOOK: Copy the storybook for each student. Color and cut out the pages along the dashed lines. Staple them together in numerical order.

BEFORE READING

1. Read the following words from the word family *-ig* that appear in the story: *big, pig, rig, fig, twig, jig, sprig, wig, jiggedy-jig*.
2. Review any unfamiliar words in the story.

AFTER READING

1. Discuss the story. What *-ig* words do the students remember?
2. Look through the story. Find and circle each *-ig* word.

MORE ACTIVITIES

1. Learn how to dance a jig. Why is this such a fun dance?
2. Bring in a fig for students to examine. Cut it open and look at the seeds. Then share fig cookies as a snack. (Check for allergies first!)

7

Jiggedy-jig, Big Pig!
You look fine in your wig!

Word Family -ill Story

The Bill from the Mill

2

Jill ran up the hill to the old, stone mill.

4

"Your bill is too high!" cried Jill. "But I still need your skill."

3

She had her bill, which she set on the sill.

6

" I will raise dill to trade at your mill," said Jill. "That's what I will do!"

8

NOTES TO TEACHERS AND PARENTS

DIRECTIONS TO MAKE THE BOOK: Copy the storybook for each student. Color and cut out the pages along the dashed lines. Staple them together in numerical order.

BEFORE READING

1. Read the following words from the word family *-ill* that appear in the story: *Jill, hill, mill, bill, sill, fill, till, dill, will.*
2. Review any unfamiliar words in the story.

AFTER READING

1. Discuss the story. What *-ill* words do the students remember?
2. Look through the story. Find and circle each *-ill* word.

MORE ACTIVITIES

1. Bring in a bottle of dill to pass around the class. Talk about what foods taste good flavored with dill.
2. How does a mill work? Explore in books or on the Internet. What does a miller do?

5

"What can we do to fill my till, Jill?" asked the miller.

7

"I will still pay your bill—I will!" said Jill.

2

The king is sad. What thing can we do to help the king?

4

We can ring the bells, too. We will swing them back and forth.

1

Singing
for the King

3

I know! We can all sing! We can sing about spring.

6

Our music has zing. The king starts to swing back and forth.

8

NOTES TO TEACHERS AND PARENTS

DIRECTIONS TO MAKE THE BOOK: Copy the storybook for each student. Color and cut out the pages along the dashed lines. Staple them together in numerical order.

BEFORE READING

1. Read the following words from the word family *-ing* that appear in the story: *king, thing, sing, spring, ring, swing, ping, ding, zing, fling.*

2. Review any unfamiliar words in the story.

AFTER READING

1. Discuss the story. What *-ing* words do the students remember?

2. Look through the story. Find and circle each *-ing* word.

MORE ACTIVITIES

1. Plan a spring fling! What things can you do to celebrate spring?

2. Hand out small bells and have students ring them as they sing a song together.

5

Ping! say the little bells. Ding! say the big bells.

7

We will have a fling as we bring our spring music to the king!

2

It's hard to hide
when you're very wide.

4

And in the tide,
I can't hide at all!

Word Family -ide Story

The Wide Elephant

1

3

Behind this slide, I show
on each side!

6

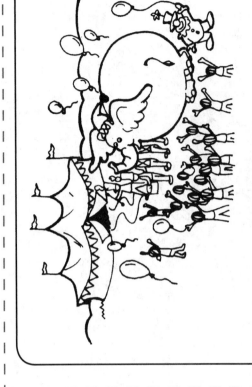

I want to stride with elephant pride in the big parade.

8

NOTES TO TEACHERS AND PARENTS

DIRECTIONS TO MAKE THE BOOK: Copy the storybook for each student. Color and cut out the pages along the dashed lines. Staple them together in numerical order.

BEFORE READING
1. Read the following words from the word family *-ide* that appear in the story: *hide, wide, slide, side, tide, ride, stride, pride*.
2. Review any unfamiliar words in the story.

AFTER READING
1. Discuss the story. What *-ide* words do the students remember?
2. Look through the story. Find and circle each *-ide* word.

MORE ACTIVITIES
1. Make circus posters that will help the elephant's pride! Show him as the star of the circus.
2. Brainstorm other *-ide* words. Have the students write a new story about the wide elephant.

5

But I don't want to hide.
I want to ride on the circus train.

7

Why hide if you are wide?
Instead, have pride!

Tonight, we will dine under the pine.

I will line up our plates. Here is yours, and there is mine.

Word Family -ine Story

Under the Pine

It will be a fine way to dine! Please come at half past nine.

6

Then we will eat grapes
right off the vine!

8

Notes to Teachers and Parents

DIRECTIONS TO MAKE THE BOOK: Copy the storybook for each student. Color and cut out the pages along the dashed lines. Staple them together in numerical order.

BEFORE READING

1. Read the following words from the word family *-ine* that appear in the story: *dine, pine, fine, nine, line, mine, vine, shine.*
2. Review any unfamiliar words in the story.

AFTER READING

1. Discuss the story. What *-ine* words do the students remember?
2. Look through the story. Find and circle each *-ine* word.

MORE ACTIVITIES

1. What foods grow on vines? Make a list together as a class.
2. Bring in toasted pine nuts for students to share and taste. (Check for food allergies first!) Would mice like to eat these?

5

We will eat fine cheese
and pine nuts.

7

The moon will shine all night
as we dine.

2

We are setting up a shop. We will sell our vegetable crop.

4

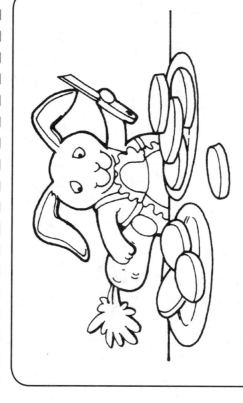

Flop will chop the top vegetables to sell.

1

Word Family -op Story

The New Shop

3

Pop will mop the floor.

6

"Our crop is so good it will make you hop! Drop by today!"

5

We will stop people and tell them about our shop.

8

NOTES TO TEACHERS AND PARENTS

DIRECTIONS TO MAKE THE BOOK: Copy the storybook for each student. Color and cut out the pages along the dashed lines. Staple them together in numerical order.

BEFORE READING
1. Read the following words from the word family -*op* that appear in the story: *shop, crop, Pop, mop, Flop, chop, top, stop, hop, drop, bop.*
2. Review any unfamiliar words in the story.

AFTER READING
1. Discuss the story. What -*op* words do the students remember?
2. Look through the story. Find and circle each -*op* word.

MORE ACTIVITIES
1. Make signs for the rabbits' new shop! Cut out vegetable pictures from magazines to decorate the signs. Price the vegetables for a money-lesson tie-in.
2. Read "The Tale of Peter Rabbit" or another Beatrix Potter story about rabbits. Find the -*op* words in the story.

7

Look at all the rabbits hop and bop to our shop!

The old mouse had once been young and bold.

2

He hid the gold in a fold of an old drape.

4

Word Family -old Story

The Old Mouse's Gold

1

He moved into a cold, old house. There he found some gold.

3

6

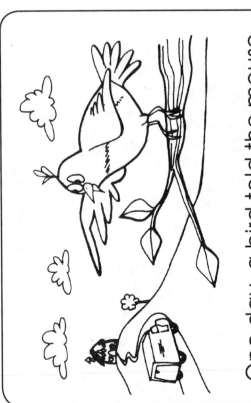

"No time to scold," said the mouse to the bird. "Help me move the gold!"

8

NOTES TO TEACHERS AND PARENTS

DIRECTIONS TO MAKE THE BOOK: Copy the storybook for each student. Color and cut out the pages along the dashed lines. Staple them together in numerical order.

BEFORE READING

1. Read the following words from the word family *-old* that appear in the story: *old, bold, cold, gold, fold, sold, scold, told.*
2. Review any unfamiliar words in the story.

AFTER READING

1. Discuss the story. What *-old* words do the students remember?
2. Look through the story. Find and circle each *-old* word.

MORE ACTIVITIES

1. What would the students buy if they found a chest of gold? Each student can buy one thing.
2. Have a treasure hunt. Hide gold-wrapped chocolate coins. Hand out treasure maps for the students to follow.

5

One day, a bird told the mouse that the old house was sold.

7

They bought a castle with all of his gold, so I'm told.

The music went, "Boom, boom, boom!"

The jet went, "Zoom, zoom, zoom!"

Word Family -oom Story

Boom!
Vroom!
Zoom!

The car went, "Vroom, vroom, vroom!"

6

I would sweep from the start of
the day until the night's gloom!

8

NOTES TO TEACHERS AND PARENTS

DIRECTIONS TO MAKE THE BOOK: Copy the storybook for each student. Color and cut out the pages along the dashed lines. Staple them together in numerical order.

BEFORE READING
1. Read the following words from the word family *-oom* that appear in the story: *boom, vroom, zoom, broom, gloom, room.*
2. Review any unfamiliar words in the story.

AFTER READING
1. Discuss the story. What *-oom* words do the students remember?
2. Look through the story. Find and circle each *-oom* word.

MORE ACTIVITIES
1. Assign each student a sound—boom, vroom, or zoom. Have everybody make their noise for 15 seconds. Follow with one minute of complete silence. Talk about noises in a city.
2. Make a collage of things in the world that make noise—traffic, boats, jets, trains, etc.

5

I wish I had a broom
to sweep up every zoom!

7

How can there be room in the air
for all these booms, vrooms,
and zooms?

Larry the Loon wanted to fly to the moon.

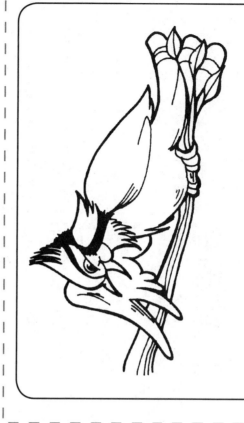

"I am sure you will get to the moon soon," nodded Ray.

Word Family -oon Story

Larry the Loon

"I will leave at noon," he told his friend Ray Jay.

6

"What a boon it will be to get to the moon," crooned Larry.

8

NOTES TO TEACHERS AND PARENTS

DIRECTIONS TO MAKE THE BOOK: Copy the storybook for each student. Color and cut out the pages along the dashed lines. Staple them together in numerical order.

BEFORE READING
1. Read the following words from the word family *-oon* that appear in the story: *loon, moon, noon, soon, spoon, boon, croon[ed], swoon.*
2. Review any unfamiliar words in the story.

AFTER READING
1. Discuss the story. What *-oon* words do the students remember?
2. Look through the story. Find and circle each *-oon* word.

MORE ACTIVITIES
1. Learn more about the moon. How far away is it? Why can't birds fly to the moon?
2. Go to a bird Web site or find a recording of a loon song for the class to hear.

5

Larry packed his fork and spoon. He wanted to eat green cheese on the moon.

7

He flew so far that he started to swoon. But that silly loon Larry never got to the moon!

Mother Bear said, "Time for a bath, Little Cub."

But Mother Bear said, "Into the tub, Little Cub!"

Word Family -ub Story

Little Cub's Bath

Little Cub said, "I want to look under this shrub."

6

"If you get clean, you can play in the tub with your new sub," she added.

8

NOTES TO TEACHERS AND PARENTS

DIRECTIONS TO MAKE THE BOOK: Copy the storybook for each student. Color and cut out the pages along the dashed lines. Staple them together in numerical order.

BEFORE READING
1. Read the following words from the word family -*ub* that appear in the story: *Cub, shrub, tub, rub, scrub, sub, rub-a-dub-dub[bed], nub.*
2. Review any unfamiliar words in the story.

AFTER READING
1. Discuss the story. What -*ub* words do the students remember?
2. Look through the story. Find and circle each -*ub* word.

MORE ACTIVITIES
1. Do the students remember their favorite tub toys from when they were little? Make a list.
2. Baby bears are cubs. What are the names of other baby animals?

5

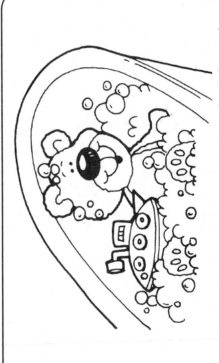

"I want you to rub and scrub away all that dirt."

7

Little Cub rub-a-dub-dubbed his fur to a nub just so he could play with his yellow sub!

Little Bug and Little Slug looked
for a new home.

"Look at this snug little house!"
said Little Bug.

Word Family -ug Story

A Snug New Home

They found an old mug.
Someone had thrown it away.

6

They brought a table, a jug, and two little mugs.

NOTES TO TEACHERS AND PARENTS

DIRECTIONS TO MAKE THE BOOK: Copy the storybook for each student. Color and cut out the pages along the dashed lines. Staple them together in numerical order.

BEFORE READING
1. Read the following words from the word family *-ug* that appear in the story: *Bug, Slug, mug, snug, tug, rug, jug, dug.*
2. Review any unfamiliar words in the story.

AFTER READING
1. Discuss the story. What *-ug* words do the students remember?
2. Look through the story. Find and circle each *-ug* word.

MORE ACTIVITIES
1. Have each student bring in a favorite mug from home. Put the mugs on display.
2. Learn more about bugs and slugs. How are they different? How are they alike?

8

5

They moved in. They had to tug the rug into place.

7

Little Bug dug a garden. Little Slug took a nap. Welcome home!

Sasha the Thrush was a pretty little bird.

"Sasha is such a pretty thrush!" gushed the other birds.

Word Family -ush Story

Thrush in a Rush

Every day, she would brush her feathers. Then she would put on her hat.

6

One day, it snowed. Sasha was
in a big rush. She slipped.
She fell in the slush!

8

NOTES TO TEACHERS AND PARENTS

DIRECTIONS TO MAKE THE BOOK: Copy the storybook for each
student. Color and cut out the pages along the dashed lines. Staple
them together in numerical order.

BEFORE READING
1. Read the following words from the word family *-ush* that appear
   in the story: *thrush, brush, gush[-ed], blush, hush, rush, slush, crush
   [-ed], mush.*
2. Review any unfamiliar words in the story.

AFTER READING
1. Discuss the story. What *-ush* words do the students remember?
2. Look through the story. Find and circle each *-ush* word.

MORE ACTIVITIES
1. Talk about winter days. What makes snow? What happens to
   make slush?
2. Read about the thrush. What does a thrush look like? What does
   a thrush's song sound like? Where does the thrush live?

5

Sasha would blush. "Oh, hush!"
she would say.
But she loved to hear
their nice words.

7

Her feathers were wet.
Her hat was crushed.
"I look like a bowl of mush!"
chuckled the little thrush.